GETTING AMERICA BACK TO WORK

Stewart Acuff and Richard A. Levins

Tasora

Cover and text design by CD Design, Ltd.

ISBN 978-1-934690-27-7
LCCN 2010924580

Steve Sack's cartoons are reprinted with
permission of the *Minneapolis Star Tribune*.

Chapter 13 was adapted from earlier work
co-authored with Courtney Pecquex.

Tasora Books
5120 Cedar Lake Road
Minneapolis, Minnesota 55416
952-345-4488

Distributed by Itasca Books
Printed in the USA
www.itascabooks.com

dedication

This book is dedicated to the leaders and activists of the Utility Workers Union of America, especially President Mike Langford whose vision is leading us to a brighter future.

And to my family whose patience and love sustain me: Mary, Sam, Sydney, Dad.

And to the memory of Bob Arnold.

And to all I've organized with and campaigned with over the years who inspired many of the ideas in this book and influenced all my work, including but not limited to Larry Cohen, Leo Gerard, Tim Waters, Ed Sabol, Stan Johnson, Fred Azcarate, Sarah and Fred McKenzie, Patrick and Merwyn Scott, Courtney Pecquex, Bill Fletcher, Sharon Pinnock, James Gibbs, Cecil Roberts, Andy Levin, Si Kahn, Charlie Fleming, Beth Levie, Don Slaiman, Dave Eckstein, Ed Tynes, Ken Johnson, Jerry Acosta, Jimmy Hyde, Ken Zinn, Rose Ann DeMoro, Brad Burton, Bob King, Cindy Estrada, Elizabeth Bunn, Julie Kushner, Bob Madore, Jim Evans, Stephen Windwalker, Paul Booth, Jim Schmitz, Joe Hunt, Bernie Evers, Greg Junemann, Benetta Mansfield, Kirk Brungard, Alan Freeman, Bernie Pollack who first got me writing in the progressive blogosphere and who got my first few pieces published, and to my first mentor, Dr. John Galliher of the University of Missouri who taught me how to think, and to all the rest of you who know who you are and what you gave to me.

Stewart J. Acuff
April 2010

GETTING AMERICA
BACK TO WORK

There was once a time when the ordinary American could expect Washington to watch out for his or her best interests. Here's what the U.S. Supreme Court said on January 21, 2010, when it ruled that corporations can shovel even more money into politics than they were already doing:

> We now conclude that independent expenditures, including those made by corporations, do not give rise to corruption or the appearance of corruption.... The appearance of influence or access, furthermore, will not cause the electorate to lose faith in our democracy....We should celebrate rather than condemn the addition of this [corporate] speech to the public debate.

In other words, Washington, with the blessing of the Supreme Court, has hung the ordinary American out to dry.

There was also a time when the ordinary American could depend on our free market system to reward his or her individual hard work with a decent living. Look at what Alan Greenspan, former Director of the Federal Reserve, said to Congress as part of his apology for trusting free markets to guide the banks: "I have found a flaw. I don't know how significant or permanent it is. But I have been very distressed by that fact."

He's been distressed? How about the millions and millions of hard-working Americans who have lost their jobs, lost their homes, and lost their hope because they trusted our economic system to treat them fairly?

What's going to save the ordinary American, trapped between a government buried in corporate cash and a market system that even its greatest supporters are starting to doubt? This little book gives you the answer in one word: Power.

Power is how you get things. Power is how you change things and make things happen. There are two forms and sources of power. The first is lots of organized money. That is the kind of power the Financial Elite have used to bring the rest of us to our knees. The other source and form of power is lots of people: organized, mobilized, united, and taking action.

That's what will save the ordinary American. Lots of ordinary Americans. Working together.

A DECADE OF DISASTER FOR WORKING AMERICANS

chapter 1

PUNCHiNG OUT

Maybe you are out of work as you read this. Surely, you know someone who is, maybe a family member or close friend. The dimensions of this tragedy are something most of us have not seen during our lifetime. Something like one in five American workers is officially unemployed, is among the so-called "underemployed," or has given up on ever finding work.

The consequences of so many people out of work are overwhelming. Millions of American families can't make their credit card payments. Foreclosures and underwater mortgages are becoming the rule rather than the exception. One in eight Americans is on food stamps. Forty-seven million of us go without health insurance. Retirement dreams have become retirement nightmares.

Our Decade of Disaster has caught up with us:

- The first decade of the twenty-first century brought zero job growth. How bad is that? Every decade since World War II has ended with at least 20 percent more jobs than it began with.
- Income for working and middle class families has been stagnant since 1980. Since 2000, that income has actually declined.
- Family wealth has tanked.

Put another way, during the Decade of Disaster, America officially stopped working for ordinary Americans. Instead, America worked only for a handful of unbelievably rich, unimaginably powerful individuals. Jobs went off-shore, factories were closed, debt replaced paychecks, and tax breaks went to the super-rich.

We didn't just fall into this mess. For the last 30 years, America's working families have endured an assault by the Financial Elite specifically designed to slash our wages and benefits, lower our standard of living, and shift wealth and power from those of us in the middle and at the bottom to those at the top.

So here we are, in the middle of the biggest economic disaster most of us have ever seen, with two big jobs on our hands. First, we need to get Americans back to work. Second, we need to get America back to working for ordinary Americans. We can't do one without doing the other. How do we turn things around?

We must begin by recognizing that our economic problems are the result of *intentional, sustained, strategic* public policy–bad public policy cooked up by the Financial Elite and their henchmen. The good news is that in a democracy people can change public policy. That's what this book is about–how we change public policy to get people back to productive work and to get America's economy working for working families.

We must understand; then act. The first part of this book lays out the economics behind the Decade of Disaster. We explain the relationship between wealth and power and why we have to build more power to change things. Don't let the word "economics" scare you–we left the gobbledygook at the university and wrote in kitchen table language. Then comes the action part. We will show you how to put more power in the hands of working families. Using that power wisely and strategically is the key to getting America back to work.

chapter 2

America works, but only for the Financial Elite. Who are they? When most of us think of rich people, we think of the power shopper down the street. That person, just like you, is a pauper compared to our real kings and queens. Look at these numbers and you will see why:

- In 2007, 14,588 people in the United States, about the same number as live in a medium-sized rural community, averaged $35 million per year. Compare that to *your* paycheck.

- Even though the economy was called "fundamentally sound" during 2002-2006, the Financial Elite raked in three out of every four dollars of America's income growth. The rest of us saw virtually no income growth at all.

- The average person on the 2009 _Forbes_ list of the 400 wealthiest Americans was worth over $3 billion. How much is that? Three billion dollars is a stack of one dollar bills over two hundred miles high.
- The federal budget deficit is projected to be something like $1.6 trillion. The Forbes 400 could stage a fund raiser that would come close to paying that off without inviting anyone but themselves.

There is no way a person can spend that kind of money on cars, houses, boats, and college degrees. So what else does membership in this most exclusive club bring? Power. Power to get around rules that most of us must live by. Power to go way beyond that; power to change the rules most of us must live by. This is what we mean when we say things like "money talks" or joke about the Wall Street Golden Rule: "He who has the gold rules." It is what Senator Richard Durbin meant when he said, "And the banks–hard to believe in a time when we're facing a banking crisis that many of the banks created–are still the most powerful lobby on Capitol Hill. And frankly they own the place."

It is one thing to own a house, and quite another to own Capitol Hill. This, in short, is the difference between what the ordinary person, even the ordinary millionaire, can buy, and what our economic royalty can buy.

Many people, with good reason, think it's outrageous that so few people should be so unbelievably rich while so many others dwell in poverty. Some of these people are motivated by religious concerns, others by a simple sense of fairness.

We will respectfully put those concerns aside and ask only this question, "Is vast wealth, concentrated in a very few hands, good for the economy?" The answer is, "No, it is not." Our economic history shows that the Financial Elite do a great job of feathering their own nests and a terrible job of running a middle class economy. If we are going to get America back to working for ordinary Americans, we will need to get money and power back into *our* hands.

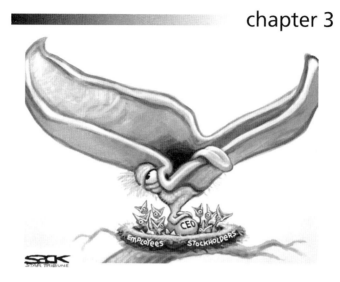

chapter 3

We've always had a Financial Elite. What changes is how much money and power they control. Professors Piketty and Saez at the University of California have put together information that allows us to see how the top one percent of Americans has fared in the United States for almost 100 years. Their studies are summarized in the graph titled, "The Rise and Fall of the Middle Class."

Notice that the Financial Elite have taken as much as 23.9 percent of the total income earned by Americans and as little as 9 percent. The lower numbers are best if you want a middle class economy. Money and power are spread among more Americans when the top one percent has a smaller piece of the pie.

Notice, too, that there is a distinct, long-term pattern in the numbers. They are very high in the years right before the Great Depression. They move dramatically toward a middle class economy right after World War II and stay there for several decades. Beginning around 1980, things start turning away from the middle class ideal and end up close to where they were during the run-up to the Depression.

What all this means is that a person growing up in the 1950's and 1960's grew up in a very different economy than the one today's young people face. The power that money brings was spread around in ways that helped most of the people most of the time during the mid-twentieth century. Things are very different now. Far fewer people call the shots, and they call those shots for their own benefit.

If we want an America that works for ordinary Americans, the graph shows it won't happen on its own. We will need power in the hands of people–working people and middle class Americans. To make that happen, we will need to find a way to put a greater share of our total income in the hands of ordinary Americans.

The Rise and Fall of the Middle Class

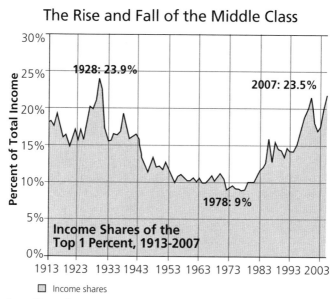

Source: Piketty and Saez, Quarterly Journal of Economics, 2003, series updated to 2007.

The income share of the top one percent is the highest it has been since the Great Depression.

The years with a lower share for the top one percent are better for the middle class.

MONEY TALKS

Are you one of the millions of Americans who have been stuck with ridiculous fees for overdrawing your checkbook by a dollar or two? Have you paid credit card companies over 20 percent, even though the government is giving the bank that issued your card money that is virtually free? Are you as mad as we are that our tax money bailed out giant investment banks, and now the same clowns who caused our economic collapse are raking in multi-million dollar bonuses?

How do they get away with this nonsense? Shouldn't there be a law or something to keep this from happening? Read what the watchdog group Public Citizen reported in 2009:

More than 900 former federal employees, including

70 former members of Congress, have gone to work as lobbyists for the financial services sector this year, Public Citizen has found. Those who have passed through the revolving door between Congress and the financial industry include a former speaker of the House, two former Senate majority leaders, and two former House majority leaders. The industry also has showered Congress with more than $42 million in campaign contributions in the past year, aiming at members of the banking committees.

There are 535 members of Congress, so that puts at least one lobbyist at every door with plenty more in reserve. On top of that, the average member of Congress could look forward to over $78,000 to help them get re-elected. That, good friend, is money talking. It's beyond talking. Money is hollering so loudly that your voice won't be heard.

But that's just banking and finance talking. How about energy? Does it seem odd that pump prices are a quarter or more higher on the drive home than they were when you left for work in the morning? Don't record profits by the companies selling gasoline and heating oil mean that you are paying too much?

Money talks. On June 19, 2009, the Business Section of the *Minneapolis Star Tribune* ran a story called, "Oil industry gushes money for lobbying." In just three months, the industry spent $44.5 million lobbying Congress and federal agencies. The year before they spent $129 million, but that record was sure to be broken. The article noted, "The investment appears to be paying off." You can't put it any clearer than that. If you control the rules of the game, you will always win.

The same article noted that there was one industry out-spending even the oil barons. Drug makers and health products companies spent $66.6 million to make sure they had their way with consumers. Apparently, money talks in the most literal way for these folks. According to the *New York Times* (November 15, 2009): "Statements by more than a dozen lawmakers were ghostwritten, in whole or in part, by Washington lobbyists working for Genentech, one of the world's largest biotechnology companies." The story goes on to say that, "The lobbyists were remarkably successful in getting the statements printed in the Congressional Record under the names of different members of Congress."

Who's paying for all this? You are. Every time you get whacked with an overdraft fee, gouged by a credit card, taken at the gas pump, or bankrupted by a medical bill, you give the Financial Elite money that will be used against you. That's the way it is, and that's the way it's going to be, as long as money and power stay where they are.

chapter 5

Having too much money in too few hands causes all sorts of problems for our economy. The *Wall Street Journal* gave a good example in a story entitled, "Pay of Top Earners Erodes Social Security" (July 21, 2009).

The more you earn, the more you pay into Social Security. However, there is a limit on how much of your wages are paid into the system. In 2009, that limit was $106,800. Neither you nor your employer is required to pay any more into Social Security once you make more than the $106,800 limit. For ninety percent of American wage earners, this means nothing. They pay part of every dollar they earn into Social Security because they make less than the limit.

There is another group, however, that makes more than

$106,800 per year, sometimes a lot more. The *Wall Street Journal* found that wages for these "highly compensated employees" were growing at a much faster rate than those for everyone else. Because of this, an increasing share of total wages paid in the United States was exempt from Social Security payments. The highly compensated wage earners were getting twice the raises that everyone else was getting, so their share of total income was on the rise. It had been 28 percent in 2002 and was up to 33 percent by 2007. This widening income gap meant that the government collected Social Security payments on a shrinking share of total wages.

As more money goes into the hands of the very wealthy, less is available to fund the retirement system the rest of us depend on. If all wages were subject to Social Security payments, the system would have another $115 billion per year coming in. Instead of going bust in 2037, as some claim it will, the system would be good for at least another 75 years.

There are two ways to fix this problem. The first is to require payments on all wages, no matter how high. The second is to redo our economy so most of the people have most of the money. That way, there wouldn't be so much income exempted from payments. In our view, only the second will work.

Here's why we think that way. Trying to leave the pay scale alone and changing the Social Security ceiling will work in theory, but it doesn't have even the smallest chance of happening. If we leave the pay scale alone, we leave the power base alone. The powerful will do what they want and there is not much we can do about it. A person worth billions has no interest in retiring on Social Security. On the other hand, if we somehow put most of the money in the hands of most of the people, power will shift toward valuing the retirement system that almost all of us will use. Whatever system we use to fund it will secure its future.

Americans want and deserve a strong Social Security system. The problem is not the laws. The problem is the imbalance of power brought about by the inequality of our income distribution.

chapter 6

A few weeks before Christmas of 2009, the citizens of Minnesota got some bad news. They already had endured steep cuts in essential services for a few years, but that wasn't enough. They needed another billion dollars to make ends meet. What to do? The governor and his staff immediately went hunting for more services to eliminate and more people to lay off. As far as they were concerned, filling the gap with additional tax revenue was out of the question.

Anyone reading *Forbes* a few months earlier would have seen that there were six people living in the Twin Cities, each of whom was worth more than one billion dollars. One of them in particular could have written a billion dollar check and still have more than the average person on the *Forbes* 400 list. Why not ask these folks, and the many other wealthy people who didn't quite make the list, to help out?

There are two ways to look at taxes. One is the now popular concept that taxes are a "burden" that should be reduced at all cost. The second is that they are essential to funding services that allow ordinary Americans to thrive. If you hold the first view, you will choose laying off teachers and police officers instead of raising taxes. If you hold the second view, you will not be willing to sacrifice so much in order to protect the super-wealthy. You will favor tax increases, but you will pay close attention to who pays the higher taxes.

The Financial Elite have enough influence to force a tax system that protects them at everyone else's expense. We have already seen that most of the income going to the super-rich is exempt from Social Security payments. This is just the tip of the iceberg.

Our Federal income tax system protects the super-rich on an increasingly grand scale. The current maximum federal income tax rate is 35%. Most of the very rich pay a lower rate on much of their income. Stock dividends are treated as capital gains and are, therefore, taxed at less than half the regular rate. As a result, someone like Warren Buffett some-times pays a smaller percentage of his income as Federal taxes than do many of the people working in his offices.

It hasn't always been this way. During the heyday of the middle class, Federal income tax rates were many times higher. When President Reagan took office, the maximum Federal tax rate was 70%. Even that was low compared to the 91% top rate during the 1950's. In fact, the last time our maximum Federal tax rate was as low as it is now was, you guessed it, during the run-up to the Depression. During those years, the maximum rate was 25%.

When Federal tax rates get cut, the middle class struggles to maintain the services they need. As a result, many of the shortfalls get passed along to states, then to local governments. Here, you find taxes that truly burden working people: sales taxes and property taxes. Compared to regular folks, the super-rich spend a much smaller part of their income buying clothes and groceries. A super-rich person has a much smaller percentage of his or her wealth tied up in his or her house. The super-rich therefore pay a lower percentage of their income as these types of taxes. A report released by the Institute on Taxation and Economic Policy on November 18, 2009, said:

> The study's main finding is that nearly every state and local tax system takes a much greater share of income from middle- and low-income families than from the wealthy. That is, when all state and local income, sales, excise and property taxes are added up, most state tax systems are *regressive*.

The simple fact of the matter is that our tax system works to increase the gap between the super-rich and everyone else. Because it increases that gap, it weakens the middle class. It is one thing to recognize that our tax system is stacked against the middle class, and another to put it back to where it favors working people. The tax system won't change itself. The rich and powerful like it just the way it is, thank you very much. The tax system needs to change, but it will only happen when ordinary Americans are once again powerful enough to force that change.

chapter 7

'Here He comes. WHO WANTS To BReak the BAD News?'

"Do the Rich Save More?" is the title of a study done for the National Bureau of Economic Research in 2000. The answer was hardly surprising: "The rich, indeed, save more." Those at the top of the income scale the researchers studied saved half of their income. Researchers didn't have data on the absolute highest incomes, but it is reasonable to think that the Financial Elite save an even larger fraction of what they bring in. We don't need to tell you that the rest of us don't come anywhere close to saving at that rate. A great many Americans are lucky to save anything at all.

To save money means to not spend it right away on necessities like clothing, food, and medical bills. For most of us, that's a good thing. It means we can set something aside for a rainy day, buying a car, putting the kids through college, or retirement. We will still spend the money, but just not right now. Nothing wrong with that. But what if you were making $35 million per year and saving $25 million? What would you do with that money? One thing for sure, you wouldn't buy shoes and groceries with it.

Warren Buffett took some of his savings and bought the Burlington Northern Santa Fe Railroad. We're not talking about buying a ticket to visit Grandma here. He put down the better part of $30 billion and bought the whole kit and kaboodle, lock, stock and barrel. The business press called his move an "investment," but it didn't create one single new job. The same railroad operated in the same way both the day before he bought it and the day after he bought it. The *New York Times* got it right when they said, "Buffett Bets Big on Railroad's Future." His so-called "investment" was merely a bet.

The conventional economic story is that we need super-rich people so they can invest in factories that give the rest of us jobs. That's one thing they could do with it, but they're not obligated. They could also get rich by making Buffett-style bets. They can bet on sub-prime mortgages, on grain prices, on currency exchanges, and on gold futures. All fun stuff, but none of it puts anyone to work. So which have they been doing lately? The graph in this chapter shows dividend payments and earnings retained for growth by corporations from 2000 to 2008. More and more, the managers and directors of major corporations are choosing to take the money out as dividends instead of leaving it in to fuel their businesses.

This is what happens when there is too much money in too few hands. For starters, too much money is hoarded by people who can't spend it. Meanwhile, those who would spend it don't have it. This weakens the economy and makes investors less willing to sink money into job-creating projects. As job-creating investments fall off, working people have less to spend, so further productive investments seem even less attractive. The economy looks more and more like a casino for the rich and a nightmare for everyone else. Paul Volker, a Presidential advisor as close as anyone to big time finance, was quoted in the *New York Times* (January 10, 2010) as saying there was not "one shred of evidence" that any investment built on so-called "innovative financial instruments" has led to economic growth.

Remember when President Bush decided to solve our economic problems by giving out checks to everyone? After some discussion, they decided that some people were so rich they shouldn't get a check. Fed Chairman Ben Bernanke appeared on NBC's Today Show (January 18, 2008) and said, "I think there is good evidence that cash that goes to low and moderate income people is more likely to be spent in the near future." He got that right. Bernanke understood that super-rich keep too much out of the spending stream. We know what happens then–the whole economy suffers.

We can fix this problem, but only if we fix income distribution first.

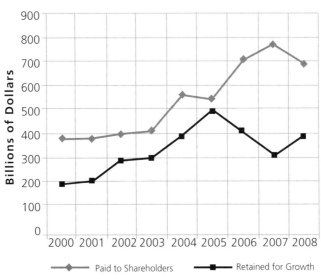

Take the Money and Run

Source: Bureau of Economic Analysis data.

Corporate profits reached record highs during the presidency of George W. Bush. Some of those profits were paid to shareholders, others were reinvested for future growth. This graph shows that "take the money and run" consistently beat "let's build for the future" as a business strategy.

chapter 8

An especially candid CEO of a US corporation told *Business Week* (April 23, 2007), "I don't have to hire one more person in the US. I don't have to invest one more dollar here, and we'll be just fine." You couldn't ask for a better example of how too much power in too few hands means big trouble for the rest of us.

The cost of so-called free trade is adding up by the day. It's a one-two punch to our middle class economy. One fist ships well-paying jobs to countries that have sub-standard wages and living conditions. The other forces lower wages in this country because everyone is told they must be "competitive" or head for the unemployment line. Fewer jobs and lower wages add up to one thing–lower purchasing power for U.S. consumers. Recent experience has shown that no amount of borrowing is going to offset this loss.

"Free" trade is not free if you're a working person.

On top of that, free trade isn't even trade. To see why, we need to go back almost 200 years to England where the theory was hatched. In those days, England was in turmoil over grain imports. Landlords benefitted from closed borders because food stayed expensive, and they could charge more for farmland. Everyone else wanted imports so they could spend more of their money on something besides food.

What has become known as free trade theory won out. The argument was simple. Suppose one country is better at producing one thing, and another is better at producing something else. Then they should both specialize in what they are best at and trade for the rest. This works just fine for agricultural products. We're better at producing grain and some other countries are better at growing coffee, so we trade grain for coffee.

Unfortunately, this has nothing to do with the modern, job-shipping version of free trade. A company that makes refrigerators in the United States and sells them to U.S. consumers decides to make them somewhere else that has cheaper wages. But they bring the refrigerators back to the United States and sell them here. What is traded? Nothing we can see. It's just a way to force labor costs down and destroy good markets along the way.

More and more people are questioning the value of the free trade idea. For example, the *New York Times* (December 29, 2007) said:

Dismal economic growth is no accident. It is the result of misguided tax, labor and social policies–including government disregard of the downsides of globalization for many Americans that have concentrated income in the hands of the few.

Here's another example. *Business Week* (February 11, 2008) wrote about how doubts are creeping into what they called "the church of free trade": "Economists are, however, noting that their ideas can't explain the disturbing stagnation in income that much of the middle class is experiencing."

Most of us already know that the goal of having "competitive labor costs" is no way to build a middle class economy. Most of us already know that we should be competing on who can have the best standard of living, not on who can work for the lowest wages. Still, free trade prevails. Why? Because free trade benefits the super-rich, pure and simple. The super-rich have the wealth and power to hire the lobbyists, make the campaign contributions, and support the so-called "think tanks" that help them get their way at everyone else's expense.

The sooner we come to our senses on trade policy, the sooner we can start the long process of rebuilding our American middle class. But we must also remember that this is not about who has the best ideas on trade. It is about who has the power to back up their ideas on trade. For now, that power is decidedly not on the side of America's working people.

chapter 9

During the last few months of his presidency, President George W. Bush joined Secretary of the Treasury Henry Paulson in announcing that the financial sky was falling. Something needed to be done. Immediately, if not sooner. No wonder there was panic in Washington and on Wall Street. Some of the country's wealthiest people were about to take a financial bath. Millions of Americans already had lost their jobs with no apparent Congressional concern, but *this* was different. These were people that mattered, and something had to be done.

The logical, free market response would have been to do what President Roosevelt did shortly after he was elected. He let the bloated banks go under, then stepped in to make things right. But that would have cost a handful of people way too much money. Instead, Congress was stampeded into borrowing $700 billion so we could "restore our financial institutions to sound footing." Panicked legislators duly fell into line and authorized TARP, the so-called Troubled Asset Relief Package, in record time.

The diagnosis of the problem was exactly what you would expect from an administration packed with bankers and millionaires. Most people would, I think, see that the problem was too many people out of work, all desperately trying to save their homes. The solution would have been to find ways to put more people back into jobs that paid middle class wages. The banks had only made things worse by luring working people into subprime mortgages and soaking them with overdraft fees. If those banks go under, good riddance. We need a banking system that works for ordinary Americans.

Of course, nothing like that happened. It can't when power is in the wrong hands. Instead, we saw a fiasco of epic proportions that mocked everything ever written in ECON 101 texts. More Wall Street bankers were appointed to clean up the mess. Instead of following the banking laws and closing those that were insolvent, the term "too big to fail" popped up in the press. Suddenly, it was all of us, not just those who had gambled and lost, who must pay for Wall Street's wild speculation binge. Accounting laws were bent so banks could essentially cook up how much their assets were worth, thereby making it impossible to trust balance sheets. In the aftermath, the banks thanked us by hiring lobbyists to oppose sensible regulation, shifted their credit card gouging operations into overdrive, slow-played legitimate loans to businesses, and handed out enormous bonuses to their top people.

All of the money we spent on the bank bailouts is basically down the tubes. We have only seen the beginning when it comes to "toxic assets"; buying all of them up will be impossible even for Congress, Inc. This should make us angry, and it should make us sad. But it should not surprise us. This is what happens when the fox guards the hen house.

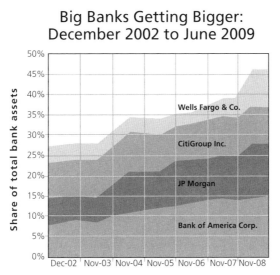

Big Banks Getting Bigger: December 2002 to June 2009

Source: Economic policy Institute, Economic Snapshot for September 9, 2009. Used with permission.

Recent years may have been tough on you, but they have been great for mega-banks. In mid-2009, the nation's four biggest bank holding companies had almost half of all bank assets.

41

A NEW
BALANCE OF POWER

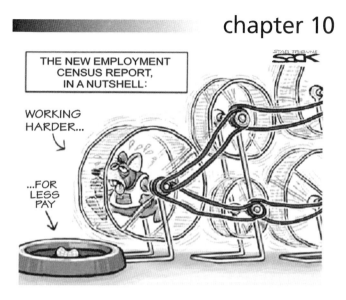

If you've gotten this far with us, you have a pretty good sense of what's going on. You know about the policies, rules, laws, and legislation that created the massive transfer of wealth and power from working families to the Financial Elite. And, we hope, you're fed up with the way things are going.

The good news in what we have written so far is this: things don't have to be this way. Together we can change America. We can put unemployed people back to work in good, productive jobs that can support families. We can raise the wages of workers in poverty level jobs. We can turn part-time work into full-time work. We can make sure everyone in America has healthcare. We can strengthen Social Security. We can strengthen families. We can protect the environment. We can rebuild our manufacturing base and industrial capacity.

In fact, to have a healthy and secure future for America, we have to do all those things. We can, but only if we work together. Humans are a social species. We live and work primarily in groups–families, towns and cities, and our workplaces. When we use the social nature of our species to lift everyone up together, to improve wages and working conditions together, to secure the future of everyone's families and kids, to win dignity on the job and respect for every worker, we are engaging in one of highest and noblest forms of human behavior. On the other hand, when we build our personal success on our neighbor's misfortune, we all lose.

This is hardly the message many of you have been taught. If you listen to the Financial Elite and the front groups they sponsor, you will think you should go it alone. Go to college. Get retrained. Work harder. Tighten your belt. Anything but organize. The graph of worker pay and worker productivity in this chapter tells the good news and the bad news for individual effort in today's economy. The good news is that individual effort has resulted in rising productivity for American workers. The bad news is that your added productivity has stopped showing up on your paycheck. The Financial Elite have become powerful enough to rig the system in ways that make you work more hours for less money.

What can we do to get Americans back to work? What can we do to get America back working for ordinary Americans? The answer to both questions is in the word "we." No one person is powerful enough to stand up to the concentration of wealth and power we see in today's America. No good idea is going to somehow pop to the surface and change the way we operate. It will be a matter of strength measured in numbers of people working together versus strength measured in dollars.

As a Minnesota farmer observed: "How big the pie is on the dinner table is only half the story of whether you will go away hungry. The other half is how big your fork is." It can't be said any more clearly than that. Unless we find ways to effectively work together, we will continue to come to the table with toothpicks while the Financial Elite come with shovels.

How do we build a big enough, powerful enough "we" that can offset the power of the Financial Elite and turn things around? There are two ways this might happen. One is organizing at the political level. The other is organizing in the market place, that is, where we work and buy things.

Productivity vs. Wage Growth

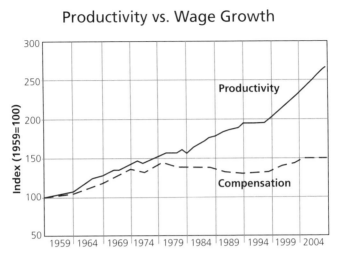

Source: Economic Policy Institute, Briefing Paper #191. Used with permission.

From 1959 to 1979, worker compensation grew with productivity. Since 1979, productivity has kept growing but hourly compensation has essentially flat-lined.

chapter 11

Here's a view of government that you don't often hear
on talk radio: "An efficient and humane society requires
both halves of the mixed system–market and government.
Operating a modern economy without both is like trying to
clap with one hand." This is a remarkable statement. Just
as remarkable is where it comes from: *Microeconomics,
Eighteenth Edition* by Paul Samuelson and William Nordhaus, one of the most respected and influential economics
textbooks of the twentieth century.

The anti-government spin machine would have you believe
the exact opposite. Don't let them fool you. The fact of the
matter is that we cannot have an economy that works for
ordinary Americans unless government plays a strong role
in creating and maintaining it. When it comes to things

like highways, police protection, and quality schools for all citizens, Professors Samuelson and Nordhaus say flat out that "adequate private production of these public goods will not occur" in unregulated free markets. The textbook also points out that a purely private economy has no built-in way to guarantee a fair distribution of income. Well-targeted government actions, such as well-targeted taxation, can prevent too much money from accumulating in too few hands and correct it when it happens.

A middle class economy is one in which the majority of citizens act together through their government to advance their common good. The opposite of a middle class economy is one in which the government is a puppet for the rich and powerful. As the income distribution tilts more and more toward the super-rich, we become closer to the puppet government model. So where are we today? Government acting for the common good of the middle class, or government owned and operated for the benefit of the Financial Elite?

We have had the pleasure of working with some legislators who are completely dedicated to the middle class ideal. We know of many more who share this view. But, by and large, these good people aren't able to get the job done when push comes to shove. Consider these examples:

- The economy goes in the tank because of a banking crisis. The response? *Borrow loads of money and give it to those very same banks.*
- Millions of people are thrown under the bus of unem-

ployment. The response? *Statements like "except for unemployment, the economy is recovering."*

- President Obama is elected to change health care by reigning in insurance companies and offering people a more efficient public option. The response? *Proposals that require everyone to buy policies from the very insurance companies that President Obama judged were the problem.*

- We are desperate for money to fund social programs that benefit the middle class. Trillions of dollars are being hoarded by the super-rich. The response? *Keep taxes low on the super-rich and borrow against our future stability.*

- The Center for Responsive Politics reported that in 2009 there were 13,426 lobbyists chasing 535 members of Congress. This army burned through $2.5 billion, and that's on top of campaign contributions. As if that weren't bad enough, in 2010 the Supreme Court struck down most of the few remaining restrictions on corporate political spending.

It is no wonder that the vast majority of Americans gives Washington a failing grade. Nonetheless, the fact remains that good government is essential if we are to be a middle class society. This brings us to a classic chicken and egg problem. Which comes first, good government or the power that supports it?

We think that the power to change government must be built outside of the political process. It must be built in the market place.

ice cream cone
(ice cream-less)

NoiSeMAKeR
(Noise-Less)

BALLoon
(AiR-Less)

CUPCAKe
(CAKe-Less)

PARTY SUPPLieS FoR CeLeBRATiNG
THe"ECONOMiC ReCoVeRY"(JoBLeSS)

What brought us out of the Great Depression? Some economic historians credit President Roosevelt's spending programs and other progressive policies. Others say it was World War II. We think both groups are partly right, but both miss an important part of the picture: labor unions. There were almost four times as many organized workers at the end of the Depression as when it began. Those organized workers apparently realized that the super-rich couldn't do anything with their money unless workers cooperated. Organized workers changed the balance of power in the Depression. They can do it again.

Labor unions are the way Americans have traditionally organized themselves in the market place. In spite of whatever the Financial Elite may have told you, there is no question that labor unions have affected our economy in positive ways. When labor union participation has been high, we have seen that the income distribution has favored working Americans. Furthermore, we have seen that when labor unions were strong, rising worker productivity translated directly into higher paychecks, not fatter Fat Cats. Sure, there were bumps in the economic road when unions were strongest, but we avoided economic catastrophes of the type we are now enduring.

On the other hand, labor union participation dramatically declined beginning in 1980. Furthermore, the pro-labor legislation gained during the 1930's has been gradually dismantled. As a result, the percentage of organized American workers has fallen back to where it was in the 1920's. This has been tough on our economy. The income distribution has tilted more toward the wealthy. Rising worker productivity has stopped translating into higher wages. The two worst economic catastrophes of the past 100 years, the late 1920's and the present, have occurred when unions were at their weakest.

The use of power in an economy involves the effective use of threats. Wealthy owners routinely threaten workers with firings, plant closings, and moving jobs overseas. On the other hand, workers' best threat is one of disrupting the orderly process of the rich getting richer. During the 1930's, there were over 20,000 strikes. The number of strikes increased during the decade as more and more workers became organized. In the peak year of 1937, there were 4,720 strikes. Think about that. Thirteen strikes each and every day, including weekends. Big Business As Usual became impossible. Wages increased, working conditions improved, legislation became more favorable to workers, and the income distribution changed so dramatically that the years immediately following World War II are sometimes called "the birth of the middle class." Today, the strike threat has all but disappeared. During 2000-2007, there were a total of 181 strikes; there were only 21 strikes during all of 2007.

The labor strikes of the 1930's were not the only time that desperate people have been forced to disrupt a system that acted against them. For example, it is hard to imagine that the sit-ins, marches and riots of the mid-1960's didn't hasten the passage of civil rights legislation. Similarly, anti-war demonstrations by young people contributed to the legislative process of ending the Vietnam War. For some, these examples are unpleasant blemishes on the history of the twentieth century. But they pale in comparison to the damage done quietly by the Financial Elite. They have off-shored millions of jobs, allowed untold thousands more to die prematurely because of lack of health care, and are now in the process of depriving an entire generation of young people of hope for prosperity.

We have thought about these issues for years. We have tried to think of ways that good policies would surface on their own in our political system just because they are the right thing to do. We've tried to think of ways individuals could somehow make it, even though the economic deck was stacked against them. Through all of this, we keep coming back to power. If you don't have power, and don't use it, you will be taken advantage of by those that do. It's therefore important for ordinary Americans reading this to ask themselves: "What power do I have?" "Is my vote enough?" "Do I need to find a way to make my day-to-day participation in the economy count?"

The Financial Elite are doing just fine. They're using their power effectively day in and day out. The only way we see for ordinary American working people to respond is by organizing into groups large enough, and strong enough, that their combined power in the market place can no longer be ignored.

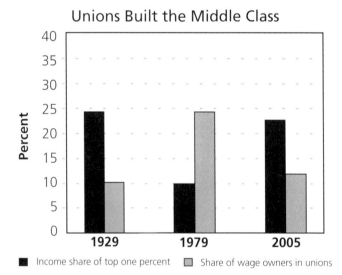

Unions Built the Middle Class

■ Income share of top one percent   ▨ Share of wage owners in unions

The American middle class was built when unions were growing and was failing when unions were in decline.

Studies have shown that 58 percent of Americans would choose a union job were it available to them. We have no doubt that America would look much better for working people if union participation were that high. Unfortunately, union participation is nowhere near that high. Only about 12 percent of American workers belong to unions. What's going on?

As the Financial Elite get more powerful, they are able to get their anti-union message out more effectively. Many of you have seen ads on television that say unions intimidate workers and want to take away their right to secret balloting. Who's behind these lies? Big Business and the Chamber of Commerce, the very groups working overtime to offshore your job and cut your paycheck. Do you really think they care about your rights?

Actually, the Financial Elite know that organized workers are trouble for them. Organized workers demand, and get, better wages and better working conditions. An economy of organized workers is one that works for the middle class, not the powerful few at the top. It costs hundreds of millions to keep working Americans in the dark, but apparently Big Business thinks their self-serving campaign is worth every penny.

Things haven't always been this way. For much of our history, America has recognized and supported organized labor. Here are a few of many examples we could use:

- President Lincoln said: *"There is no America without labor, and to fleece the one is to rob the other."*
- President Kennedy said: *"Those who would destroy or further limit the rights of organized labor–those who would cripple collective bargaining or prevent organization–do a disservice to the cause of democracy."*
- President Obama said: *"We cannot have a strong middle class without strong labor unions. We need to level the playing field for workers and the unions that represent their interests."*

As the Financial Elite have come to power, however, we are far more likely to hear something that goes beyond simple opposition to organized labor. What we hear instead is outright hysteria among those who oppose the rights of working people. A great example happened when President Obama, during his first year in office, nominated Errol

Southers to head the Transportation Security Agency. There was special urgency to get someone in the job because of a Christmas Day terrorist plot against an American air carrier.

You would think that Congress would have rushed through the nomination of this qualified individual so we could get on with the business of guaranteeing the safety of our air transportation system. Instead, Senator Jim DeMint, a Republican from South Carolina, used his senatorial privilege to place a "hold" on Southers's nomination. Why, in such an urgent time, block the nomination of a fully-qualified candidate? Senator DeMint was concerned that Southers would not come out *against* granting collective bargaining and other basic worker rights to 40,000 Transportation Security Officers. In fact, Senator DeMint went as far as saying that collective bargaining "weakens security" and would put the safety of the public at risk.

Talk about hysteria! Never in the history of this nation has a union card jeopardized national security. In fact, US Capitol Police–who protect Senator DeMint and his colleagues–are unionized. The first responders on 9/11 belonged to Firefighters and Police Unions. As the war goes on in Afghanistan, members of the Seafarers International Union continue to serve their historic role as the nation's fourth arm of defense, supplying our troops in times of war and national emergency.

Senator DeMint and his backers had much more in mind than preventing Transportation Security Officers from forming a union. Thousands upon thousands of Transportation Security Officers have bravely stood up and joined the American Federation of Government Employees. In fact, these Officers have had union representation from Day One. Because of that, they have gained some basic work place protections and have been able to counter unfair treatment. Senator DeMint was leading the charge to dismantle the gains workers had made.

Sadly, Southers withdrew and the process of filling the position dragged on. Meanwhile, we are all reminded of an important lesson: there are those who will do anything, including jeopardizing our national security by slowing the process of filling a key leadership position, to keep workers from organizing.

chapter 14

We have seen how American workers seeking to organize face anti-union hysteria in the media. As bad as that is, it is nothing compared to what awaits them in the workplace. To understand how vicious anti-union forces can be, you have to understand how workers form a union in the first place.

Workers trying to form a union must prove that a majority of their co-workers also want union representation. There are two ways this support can be demonstrated. Workers can collect the signatures of a majority of the employees. These signatures are then presented to the employer and the National Labor Relations Board (NLRB). Or, alternatively, workers can hold an election supervised by the NLRB.

Majority sign-up is easier, quicker, and leaves the process of forming the union in the hands of the workers–where it belongs. Elections, on the other hand, sound great, all-American, and democratic. But in the last 30 or so years, employers and a $4 billion-a-year industry of union busting attorneys have turned these union organizing elections into a farce of democracy. Using threats, firings, harassment, intimidation, and retaliation, employers have removed any semblance of democracy from these elections.

No matter which of the two ways workers choose to form a union, the process is refereed by the National Labor Relations Board. The Board is charged with administering the National Labor Relations Act. That act, passed in 1935, regulates workers' rights and labor relations in most of America's private sector. According to its preamble, the act was passed to encourage collective bargaining, freedom of association, and worker organization. During the past few decades, however, the Board has been doing the exact opposite of its legal mission.

For example, administrative decisions by the National Labor Relations Board have made it harder for workers to form a union through a majority sign up. Most American workers who form a union these days do so through a majority sign up process. The more traditional election system for forming a union has fallen under NLRB bias, so it should not be surprising that workers avoid it when they can. Decisions by the NLRB have also made it more difficult for workers who are illegally fired to recover back pay. Workers who come to a job intending to try to form a union face a legalized form of job discrimination. Union supporters who are illegally denied employment are treated as second-class workers.

These are not the only ways the National Labor Relations Board has gone out of its way to weaken workers' rights, especially the freedom to form unions and bargain collectively. During the time President George W. Bush was in office, his Board acted regularly to deny collective bargaining and organizing protection to millions of workers across our country and throughout our economy. They took away Labor Board coverage from many disabled workers, university and graduate employees, and others. Then, in the infamous Kentucky River and Oakwood cases, they caused as many as 8 million non-supervisory, non-management workers to be inaccurately labeled as supervisors. This action denied those Americans their right to collective bargaining coverage and any opportunity to form a union.

When the NLRB fox guards the henhouse, things get very tough for individuals trying to exercise their rights to bargain collectively. Dr. Kate Bronfenbrenner of Cornell University did a study that showed just how bad things are. Here are some of her findings from an analysis of union election campaigns supervised by the National Labor Relations Board:

- 63% of employers interrogated workers in mandatory one-on-one meetings with their supervisors about support for the union.
- 54% of employers threatened workers in such meetings.
- 57% of employers threatened to close the worksite.

- 47% of employers threatened to cut wages and benefits.
- 34% of employers fired workers.

All of this is illegal, but with trivial penalties and lax enforcement, it goes on all the time. Even if the NLRB does rule in favor of a worker, the employer can count on appeals lasting three to five years in the most serious cases.

We could go on about how the deck is stacked against working Americans, but we think you get the picture. The real question is not, "Why are so few Americans organized?" Instead, we should be asking, "How did so many muster the courage and determination to exercise their rights in such a hostile environment?"

GETTING BACK TO WORK

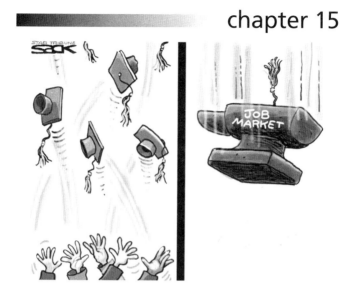

Our principal task must be getting Americans back to work. We must also get America back to working for ordinary Americans. As we have said before, the two tasks go hand-in-hand. To do one, you must do the other.

In the following chapters, we outline three broad objectives that all of us should be working towards to get our economy back on track:

- Legislation and administrative rules that level the playing field for workers trying to organize themselves in the market place.

- A green jobs program to create well-paying jobs in areas that reduce our dependence on fossil fuels.

- A reindustrialization program to rebuild our economy's manufacturing foundation.

These three programs, taken together as a package deal, will allow working Americans to both build the power they need to get things done and to strategically use that power in ways that get our economy back on track.

chapter 16

America's broad, deep middle class, indeed, the American Dream, was formed in the 20-25 years after the passage of the Wagner Act in 1935. The Wagner Act formalized the right of workers in America to freely form unions and bargain collectively. Americans recognized the value of their right to organize: between 1935 and 1955, 12 million workers formed unions. During those years, more than one in three American workers became union members. Organized workers literally bargained their way into the middle class and bargained for their share of the American Dream.

No one gave those workers a ticket to the middle class. No one gave them a guaranteed share of the pie. The middle class didn't somehow just happen. No, those workers faced exactly what today's workers face–powerful interests that are doing everything they can to promote cheap wages and poor benefits. Restoring the freedom to form unions and bargain collectively is as much a part of today's economic recovery as it was back then. Powerful, organized workers will earn more and therefore be able to buy more. Furthermore, powerful, organized workers can back policies needed to get America back to work.

We hear a lot about economic stimulus plans lately. They all involve massive borrowing and bigger government. It's time we got serious about a stimulus plan that will cost the taxpayers nothing and will work for ordinary Americans, not Wall Street. In our view, that stimulus plan is one of making organizing easier.

- Labor unions, people of faith, civic and community leaders, academics, and other Americans of good will have been working hard since about 2002 to restore workers' rights to organize in the workplace.

- Already 12 states have reformed their laws governing public employee labor relations to give state workers and others the freedom to form unions and bargain collectively--including majority sign-up.

- Very productive work is underway to change the rules in the Railway Labor Act to restore essential freedoms to workers in America's transportation industry to form unions and bargain collectively.

- Most importantly, we are close to getting the support necessary to pass the Employee Free Choice Act.

The Employee Free Choice Act has three important parts. First, it simplifies and streamlines organizing. Second, it effectively punishes employers who violate workers rights with

$20,000 civil fines and triple damage back pay for firing workers. Third, it forces the Financial Elite to bargain in good faith with unions by allowing unions to seek arbitration for recalcitrant employers. The legislation has the support of President Obama. The House of Representatives passed it 241-185 in March of 2007. Now the Financial Elite have circled their wagons in the Senate and are taking advantage of the requirement that majority support is not enough to pass legislation.

We remain hopeful that Congress will see the economic importance of the Employee Free Choice Act. We also have administrative options to get where we need to be. President Obama, Vice President Biden, and their appointees to the National Labor Relations Board control the rules on how unions can be formed. Those rules can be set to favor the Financial Elite, or they can be set to favor American workers. Either way, through Congressional or administrative action, Americans must once again be allowed to fully exercise their democratic freedoms of speech, assembly, and association so they can build the collective power to challenge the Financial Elite and get America back to work.

The obstacles before us are great, but so is the prize. Imagine an America in which forming a union was a simple, straightforward act. Imagine an America where the boss was powerless to deny your right to organize. Imagine an America in which you could bargain for a fair share of the wealth you create. That, our friends, will be an America that is back to work.

Majority Sign-Up: No Sign of Coercion

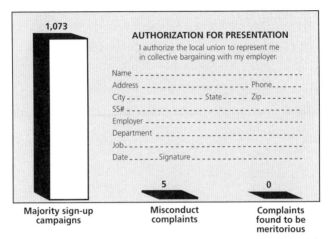

1,073

AUTHORIZATION FOR PRESENTATION
I authorize the local union to represent me in collective bargaining with my employer.

Name _____
Address _____ Phone_____
City _____ State_____ Zip_____
SS# _____
Employer _____
Department _____
Job_____
Date_____Signature_____

5

0

Majority sign-up campaigns **Misconduct complaints** **Complaints found to be meritorious**

Source: Economic Policy Institute, Economic Snapshot for August 19, 2009. Used with permission.

Industry advertising wants you to worry about union organizers "coercing" workers when secret ballots are not used. The facts say otherwise. A study of four states already allowing majority sign-up campaigns failed to turn up a single meritorious case of coercion or fraud in over 1,000 campaigns involving 34,000 employees between 2003 and 2009.

chapter 17

MIDEAST OIL DEPENDENCE

More and more Americans realize that unless we maximize the use of sustainable, domestic sources of energy, our future is threatened. At the same time, it is very hard for the average worker to care about the environment if he or she is worried about how to provide dinner for the family or pay the rent on Friday. We can make a lot of progress toward solving both of these problems–unsustainable energy and an unsustainable economy–if we get serious about creating "green jobs."

Skyrocketing energy costs, especially when that energy comes from foreign sources, is a drag on our economy. Left alone, this situation will only get worse. Our fossil fuels will one day run out. Before that happens, the cost of controlling air pollution will grow. This is one of those times when both our economy and our environment are telling us the same thing. We must tap those sources of energy that are not only sustainable but everlasting–the wind that never stops blowing across the Great Plains, the incessant pull of the tides of our oceans, the incredible energy of the sun.

Taking advantage of this everlasting energy requires skilled craftspeople to build the windmills and turbines. We will need more just like them to build and install the turbines that can be turned by the tides of the sea. Electricity created by the winds in Nebraska, North and South Dakota, and Kansas has to get to where it's needed. That requires skilled workers to build a new electricity grid and power lines. Other qualified workers will be needed to retrofit our houses, commercial buildings, and government offices in ways that conserve energy from all sources. In other words, a green energy program is also a green jobs program. The number of jobs created in rebuilding the energy foundations of our economy will be measured in the millions.

The question we need to ask is: "What kind of jobs?" Will solar collectors be built in offshore sweatshops or in American factories? Will jobs in wind turbine factories be minimum wage jobs with low benefits, or jobs with the pay and benefits that support a middle class economy? If we spend all of our time asking, "What kind of technology?" and none asking "What kind of jobs?," you can make a pretty good guess at which way things will go. Economic power will tilt our economy too far toward corporate profits and too far away from middle class jobs. The opportunity to rebuild our economy will be wasted.

Clearly, it's critical to act in meaningful ways to reduce our dependence on fossil fuels. Here, the powers that be will drag their feet as they always have done. The present situation may not be good for most of us, but it is very good for the Financial Elite. At the same time, it's critical that we are very intentional about how we create these jobs to ensure that they maximize the benefit to the overall economy and not simply to the Financial Elite. Again, this is something that won't happen on its own. We will need the power to make it happen.

How often have you been told that there is a "trade off" between a healthy economy and a healthy environment? This is simply not true. The question is not sustainable jobs *or* a sustainable environment. It is sustainable jobs *and* a healthy environment. The current power structure will take us ever farther away from that dream. A new power structure will take us toward it. Sustainable jobs for a sustainable environment. That is why labor and environmental groups have come together to form the Blue Green Alliance and the Green Jobs Initiative. This is a great start, but it will take more to get it done. It will take you.

chapter 18

During the last Great Depression, it made sense to stimulate the economy by finding ways to help consumers spend more. The things they bought were for the most part made in America, so consumption stimulated the American economy. How things have changed! Now American consumption is more likely to stimulate the economies of low-wage economies around the world. We are learning the hard way that an economy based on borrowed money and consumption without production benefits only the Financial Elite.

Creating middle class jobs is now more complicated. Surely, we need the consumption that goes with better wages. But we also need to be manufacturing the things that workers are buying. We must stop the Financial Elite from forcing American workers to compete with prison labor in China and child labor in parts of Latin America and Asia. We have to restore common sense rules governing imports and exports. In other words, our economic policies must provide incentives for investments in domestic manufacturing and penalties for oppressing workers in America and across the developing world.

American workers are some of the most skilled and productive in the world. We can build what we need here, what we use here. We can build and make here what other people need. We don't have to import cheap goods and export good jobs. Turning things around will take action by all of us. It will take a government willing to negotiate trade deals that protect workers' rights and freedoms, that honor unions, that outlaw exploitation of workers here and abroad. If our government can negotiate trade deals that protect the investments of the Financial Elite, it can negotiate trade deals that protect the economic security of the United States and its people.

Many other countries have shown how important maintaining their manufacturing base is to their economy. Countries that encourage domestic manufacturing and production and discourage worker exploitation often have higher wages and lower unemployment than we have in the United States. Countries like Canada and Germany and Sweden and Denmark and Brazil and South Africa are growing or maintaining a middle class by investing in and providing incentives for domestic manufacturing. These governments work with businesses and unions to protect middle class jobs and to protect investment internally.

When Europe came together to create a unified economic system, the European Union, they did it in a way to raise the standard of living in Portugal and Spain, not lower the standard of living in Germany and Sweden. We have been doing just the opposite.

When the United States entered World War II, we took the manufacturing capacity that had been created in Chicago and Detroit and Flint and Toledo and Akron and Pittsburgh and turned it to manufacturing the munitions and tanks and rifles and planes that the allies used to defeat Nazism, Fascism, and Japanese Imperialism. The manufacturing capacity that kept us free is now so crippled we have to wonder about what it means for our national security.

Both our economic security and our national security demand we rebuild our ability to produce more of what we consume. We can continue down the path of losing jobs, losing economic strength, and falling for the free trade con job so favored by the Financial Elite. Or, we can join together in demanding common sense policies that benefit the other 99 percent of Americans.

ENOUGH IS ENOUGH

"Freedom is never voluntarily given by the oppressor; it must be demanded by the oppressed."

— Martin Luther King Jr.

Rosa Parks
1913-2005

We've heard it said that you should never waste a crisis. Let us not waste these dark days by losing hope. Let us instead rise to the challenge before us. Let us recognize that the future of our country, the quality of life for our children and grandchildren, and the stability of our global economy hang in the balance.

Though some of us may have been divided in the past, we no longer have the luxury of division. All of us—workers, trade unionists, advocates and organizers for the poor and immigrants, environmentalists, feminists, gay rights activists, clergy and people of faith, community leaders, seekers of peace and warriors for justice—share a common challenge and a common destiny.

We are bound by a common destiny and even more strongly by common values that have guided us on a long struggle for greater freedom and justice:

- We believe that people count for more than profit or money.
- We believe that peace is better than war.
- We believe that the creation around us is worthy of our protection.
- We believe that each person and each worker is worthy of dignity and respect.

Deep down, we know these are the right beliefs to hold. We must use them to guide our struggle for human sustainability. Our environment must be sustainable. Our jobs must be sustainable. Our health must be sustainable. Our economy must be sustainable.

We have suffered through a 30-year assault on our values, on our society, on our people, on our institutions, and on our standard of living. Contrary to 4,000 years of human history, wisdom, and sacred teachings, we have been told that greed is good, that you are not your brother's and sister's keeper, that you are on your own.

We have worked harder and put in more hours for less. We have become more productive without harvesting the rewards of our effort. Our buying power has fallen. Our security is shattered. Our hopes for retirement are fading.

Enough is enough. It is time to choose.

We can continue to be driven by a Financial Elite that degrades our environment, busts our unions, ships jobs overseas, Wal-Marts our economy, and tells us we must compete for work with countries that force children to toil in the most deplorable conditions imaginable.

Or, we can bargain our way out of poverty, we can bargain the meanness out of work, we can bargain for wages that restore our buying power, and we can once again have an economy that works for ordinary Americans. Our values, not the values of greed and short-term profits, can once again guide our country.

The right choice, indeed the only choice, is clear. Together, we can do what must be done.

About the Authors

Stewart J. Acuff has been an organizer for more than 30 years. He started union organizing in 1982 as SEIU organizing coordinator in Texas where he and his team organized 12 nursing homes in two years. In 1985 Stewart went to Georgia where he founded SEIU Local 1985 and built the union up to 3000 members. In 1990 he became president of the Atlanta AFL-CIO where he organized and led the historic campaign to unionize the 1996 Olympics, labor's biggest victory ever in the South. In 2000 he went to work for the national AFL-CIO. Stewart was organizing director from 2001 to 2008. Under his tenure the labor movement grew by more than it had in a generation. Stewart developed the policy and legislation which became the Employee Free Choice Act and led the campaign to pass it. Now Stewart is Chief of Staff of the Utility Workers Union of America.

Dr. Richard A. Levins is Professor Emeritus of Applied Economics at the University of Minnesota. He is an award winning author of books about policy and market power issues affecting the food system. His articles have appeared in major newspapers across the country, in leading industry publications, and in professional journals. His writing draws upon a 25-year academic career involving both advising on-going businesses and teaching economic principles at the college level. He maintains an active practice in consulting, writing, and public speaking.